Reflections
of
Adoption

A Comprehensive Collection of Expressive Poems

To: my cousin Jacinta)

It was so good to spend time
with you after so long.

Hope you enjoy some of these.

Love always,
Sherry

Reflections of Adoption

A Comprehensive Collection of Expressive Poems

All poems created and written by:

Sharon D. Mills

Illustrated by:

Sheila Jackson

Brittany Press
Carmel, Indiana

Library of Congress Control Number: 2002090043

Published by: Brittany Press
               P.O. Box 10
               Carmel, IN 46082

http://www.BrittanyPress.com
Giftadp@aol.com

I.Title.

ISBN 0-9717324-0-X

This book was printed in the United States of America

10987654321

Second Printing March, 2002

CONTENTS

DEDICATION

I dedicate this book to my beautiful daughter, Brittany. You came to us almost 13 years ago and changed our lives forever. When I think that if there had been no adoption process we might have missed the opportunity to love and be loved by such a beautiful angel.

It has always been important to me that you be comfortable with your adoption and know that we are comfortable with it and all that it might entail. If you have questions we are here to answer them; if you have fears we are here to calm them and most importantly we are here to love you unconditionally.

Over the years when people see how close we are, I have been asked if I am afraid that you might search for your birth mom one day. My reply is that I'd be more afraid that if we tried to withhold such an important piece of your life from you (if you have the need to know it) that all the love and trust we have spent so many years building, would be jeopardized by our selfishness. Years ago, someone was unselfish enough to give us one of the best gifts we could ever receive in life. When and if it is time, I will be unselfish enough to do for you the same. My darling daughter, the choice will always be yours, but in my heart, whatever you choose I am confident that it will not lessen the love and the bond that we have spent so many years building. I love you, my daughter.

Your Mom

A special thank you to John and Margie Davies for sharing your hearts with us while we were going through the adoption process. When our daughter came to us - you shared with us a beautiful poem that touched our hearts deeply. I would now like to share my book of adoption poems with you - with the hope that your hearts may now be touched.

Thank you,
Sharon

A special thank you to Mentzer Printing Ink.

Introduction

Adoption is a wonderful gift, by which families are brought together. This book has some situations that are unique to adoption. However, many are universal. I believe that any reader will find something in this book that they will be able to relate to. There is a poem entitled: "What Is a Parent," which all parents will certainly be able to identify with.

In the reading of these poems you will see how "all" families have many similarities. The only real difference in adopted children is how they arrived at their homes. All families need the same ingredients: respectful/loving parents, respectful/loving children, the support of one another, to be heard at one time or another, and a commitment to work through the difficult times.

It is my hope that these poems will touch the hearts of many. I hope that they will prompt dialogue, initiate healing, understanding, and most of all bring families closer together.

To the adoptive parents, trust in the strength of your family's love when your children have questions. Their need to know things is no different than that of birth children wanting to know their family's history, or stepchildren who have the challenge of balancing two families.

To the adopted child, when your adoptive parents agree to share the information you're asking, trust them to know when the time is right. Also, let them know that you trust in the love you've all shared as a family and will not allow anything to destroy the life that you've all shared together. We must get over the fear that finding or adding someone new in our lives somehow lessens the amount of room we have for those whom we have always loved. The reality is there is more than enough love to accommodate everyone. Our hearts have the capacity to love far more people than we might ever imagine!

To the birthparents, to some your decision may seem like one of selfishness, but to many, we know it to be quite the opposite. Anyone, who has given life to a child and for whatever reasons, loved that child enough to let go, that he/she might be placed with people who would love and cherish him/her, should be commended. As we all know, you had a choice. So the first gift you gave your child was life and the second was a chance to live it in an environment that at the time you may not have been able to provide. Without "you" we may never have been able to hold the title of "parent".

It is my hope that we would all understand the importance of the other's position. When and if we visit the issue of re-entering a child's life or showing our support if and when a child has the need to know more - let us, at all times, weigh what our decision would mean to the child. They are life's most precious gift!

Will You Still Love Me

You've decided to adopt
oh, I think that's great
But, before you follow through
there are things to contemplate
When I keep you wide awake
for hours throughout the night
Will you still love me
When I'm not easily comforted
Will you still love me
When I break your favorite vase
Will you still love me
When I embarrass you with my behavior
Will you still love me
When your interests are not mine
Will you still love me
When I am shy and quiet instead of jovial
Will you still love me
When I want to be home, not competing in sports
Will you still love me
When I'm confused as a teenager
Will you still love me
When I follow my dreams and not yours
Will you still love me
When I marry someone not of your choosing
Will you still love me
When you answer these questions
please answer them all true
Before you take me home
to start a life with you

Gratitude

When at first it was said
I am sorry you cannot conceive
My heart could not readily
accept this truth to believe
Although I must admit
I shed so many tears
Because we're told we'll be mothers
throughout our earlier years
I pulled myself together
and said a mother I'll be
though not through my own pregnancy
would a child come unto me
And so I thank you mother
who truly cared enough
to choose for your child what was best
although it had to be tough
In making this decision
you had fears, guilt, and dread
but you were only being cognizant
of the life that lay ahead
And one day your angel may tell you
that he doesn't hold you at fault
And the decision that you have made
was certainly not for naught
So be at peace birthmother
regardless of what others may say
it was because of your decision
that I am blessed with a child today

Difficult Decisions

It was not very easy
letting go as you might think
Things just happened so fast
when I was just at the brink
of making important decisions
that would affect the rest of my life
But one thing I knew absolutely
I was too young to be somebody's wife
Then the decision became
can I do this alone
Or give my child a chance
for a more stable home
I can tell you this decision
my whole life forever changed
But I did what I felt was right
although somehow it felt strange
Some thought I was so selfish
and the decision was all about me
I sat and I cried in amazement
and thought how could this be
Giving up your child
is the hardest thing one could ever do
Please believe this decision
was truly made for you
This wasn't about fun
that I'd have if I gave you away
How much fun could it be
to have a hole in your heart everyday
I did it my child just for you
in the hopes that your life would be full
And that some special family
would treat you like their precious jewel
A mommy and daddy I sought

to protect you and meet all your needs
to nurture and truly love you
this child I too young conceived
So regardless of what others may tell you
there is something you must know
It was only through love and faith
that I was able to let you go

Be at Peace

Once there was a mother
with a child she couldn't keep
I've often sat and wondered
if this caused her to weep
I would like to say to this mother
there's no reason to shed your tears
Your child has two loving parents
who've been honored to calm her fears
So when you close your eyes
after a long and busy day
may your heart be at peace
and your doubts all washed away

The Need to Know

When we begin the process of adoption
It's important to remember
the children have no option
Yes they are blessed to live
in a home filled with love
But we must remember
they are gifts from above
These little gifts
did not just appear
There was another woman
who helped deliver them here
So please don't feel threatened
when your child to you will say
Do you think I'll ever see
the woman who birthed me one day
From the time they are children
we say ask, learn and grow
I am here to help you
with all you need to know
But when that one question
so innocently appears
We must not allow it
to cause so many fears
We say it is our desire
that our children would be whole
But when we chastise for curiosity
they question our role
The child sits and wonders
what did I do
To make mother feel angry
so sad and so blue
I handled this question
with my child you see

and the way that I see it
It's a compliment to me
Because what it showed me
is I have gained her trust
That she could feel comfortable
asking whatever she must
Our relationship was strengthened
because I did not deny
That her beginning was important
and not some terrible lie
The next time this question
just comes from nowhere
Please let your child know
that you will be there
It's not meant to hurt you
or cause you any pain
But how you respond
will determine your gain
When they ask such a question
they're not looking to go
But for many different reasons
they just have a need to know

My Own Child

Family and friends
all come to wish you well
They bring gifts and best wishes
and stories to tell
You stand there so proudly
with this bundle in your arms
And someone makes a comment
in which they meant no harm
They look at you and remark
"You know what they say"
Now that you've adopted
you may conceive your "own" one day
How could they not know
the baby that they see
is just as much your "own"
as one you birthed could ever be
Because they've not adopted
It might be hard to understand
that the love is really the same
once you touch that precious hand
If you've ever made this comment
there is something you should know
When you look in the face of a mother
we all have the very same glow
Motherhood is a blessing
regardless of how it came to be
Not conception or adoption
but mothering is the key

Privacy Please

*I know when you asked
how much did you pay?
You couldn't possibly have realized
what an insensitive thing to say
Our child is not property
or something for us to own
It's not like getting a mortgage
when buying ourselves a home
This is a little life
that's as precious as can be
So let's speak only of love
and certainly not the fee*

Please Love Me the Same

Although I tried to tell you
you chose not to believe
You thought that my motive
was only to deceive
Although to you I came first
when a second child to you was born
Things began to change
and my place in our home felt strange
Daddy the love that you show me
is just the same as before
But Mommy treats me differently
once you walk out of the door
I don't think she realizes
that all the things she says
cause me an upset stomach
each night when I go to my bed
She says things like you are my favorite
and I'm so glad that you came to be
But Daddy I can assure you
that she isn't talking to me
When I try very hard
she always calls me a quitter
And I hear in her tone
something that sounds very bitter
Although to my sibling
she will always say
good my little honey
you can try again some day
I know why you wouldn't believe this
because this side to you she doesn't show
It is always when you are not there
because she doesn't want you to know
I understand the excitement
of the birth of another
But when I was adopted
she also promised to be my mother
It shouldn't feel so different
when the things to us are said
Daddy please try to fix this
so my stomach won't hurt in my bed

Be a Winner

They didn't deserve to have you
when abuse was all they did
I'm sorry for the lonely nights
when you ran to your room and hid
They didn't deserve to raise you
when causing so much pain
It is obvious my child
this was more about selfish gain
To say to their friends look here
we're the perfect family you see
But when you tried to talk to them
they said go away and let us be
They didn't deserve to keep you
when on your knees you had to pray
Dear Lord please help me survive this
if only for another day
Dear child, I say to those parents
why'd they ever open their door
How dare they break a child's spirit
when children deserve so much more
Don't be fooled for a second
there is something they must know
To have hurt one of God's precious ones
they will certainly reap what they sowed
Now O child that you're older
don't let the pain fill your head
Take charge of your life and live
to your fullest potential instead
I promise you if you do this
you will certainly win
And no one can ever hurt you
or break your spirit again

Between You and Me

Oh, birthmother
why can't you see
that this is not a war
between you and me
Our child is the one
whom I am protecting
from the premature meeting
that you are expecting
You say I am keeping
you from your rights
Did you forget it was me
who had long sleepless nights
You made a choice
and no you shouldn't pay
there might be a relationship
in the future one day
To come into the life
of this sweet child you see
would make this a war
between you and me
Adolescence is a time
when children question their fate
And just an everyday occurrence
feels like too much on their plate
To cause more confusion
with this obstacle you see
would really not benefit
either you or me
Although I am saying
this is not the right time
I know that this child
is in your heart as well as mine
Please trust me when I tell you
that your day will come you'll see
but what's important now
is our child's stability

You say after high school or college
this I really don't know
We'll watch for the signs
when the interest he might show
to the world that he is ready
to take on deeper things
And is mature enough to handle
what all of that might bring
Right now I must finish
what I've started out to do
For it is now my job
to see this task through
Please find it in your heart
the will to understand
Your reward may come later
when our son becomes a man

Acceptance

We must say we wondered
how all of you might feel
on that very special day
when the adoption became real
Did you say to yourselves
She's not one of us
We'll just pretend
as we know that we must
Our family blood
is not in her veins
So she's not really related
except only in name
Then we say to you
bloodline should not be key
Giving love where it's needed
is what the issue should be
For so many reasons
all of which we won't explain
Love has made this our child
and not only in name
So if you all love us
as we know that you do
Accept our baby as family
because we've asked you to

Forgive Us

We were sorry to learn
that your life was filled with dread
When we made our decision
it was with the hope you'd be loved and fed
We didn't have the means
to do the things we should
Like feed, clothe, and shelter you
if we could have we certainly would
No food, no heat, no money
we were poor I guess you could say
But when we made our decision
we couldn't know the price you would pay
In hindsight it would have been better
to keep you right in our arms
To spare you the pain and the suffering
from those who could cause you such harm
Forgive us now this decision
although we did what we thought we must
We now know because of your struggle
it would have been better to have kept you with us

It's Been Good

There were birthday parties with candles
and trips and so much more
Whenever I came home from school
there was always someone at the door
When I skinned my knee
they would clean and seal it with a kiss
It brings a smile to my face
when I remember this
I went out for ice cream
and swimming down at the shore
But don't get me wrong about this
I had to do a lot more
They said you must do your homework
and be the best you can be
This is what helped me get ready
to be the child you might one day see
If you meet them please thank them
for a job I consider well done
They taught me that my life was meaningful
and not just all about fun
So don't ever question your decision
that you made for me on that day
My life has been so very full
I worked hard but also had time to play

Small Price to Pay

When at first we got the call
the news I could not comprehend
But after just a few moments
I realized our wait had come to an end
They said we have for you a baby
that it's now time for you to meet
I felt so warm all over
as if someone had turned up the heat
My emotions soon overtook me
and I turned to your father to say
Honey it looks like our waiting
will finally be over today
I want you to know little darling
when at first we held you near
nothing compared to the joy we felt
not even the anxiety or the fear
If we had to do it over
all it took to get to this day
having you now in our arms
would be but a small price to pay

No Need To Worry

They fed, bathed and clothed me
most of all showered me with love
They never failed to let me know
I was a gift from Heaven above
So you see your prayers were answered
when you looked to Heaven to say
Oh Lord please bless my decision
that I had to make on that day

Do You Ever Think of Me

I'm just sitting here thinking
do you ever think of that day
When you had a little daughter
although I did not stay
When waking up in the morning
in the mirror your features you see
Does that prompt a memory
and do you think of me
Do you wonder if I am loved
happy, safe and secure
Or is the thought of me too much
for you to even endure
When your coworker's having a party
for their child who has just turned three
With the flicker of the candles
do you ever think of me
When you're driving in your car
and see a sign that says baby on board
Do you look to Heaven
and say where is she Dear Lord
When you go on with life
and find that perfect mate
Do you tell him that you have a daughter
or convince yourself to just wait
I ask some of these questions
not to make you feel guilty you see
I ask because I sometimes wonder
Do you ever think of me

Do You Know I Think of You

I thought of you just this morning
when quickly I rolled out of bed
I went down on my knees and prayed
please make sure she's well-loved and fed
I went to a birthday party
and there were little ones playing all around
I suddenly looked up to Heaven
and said please let her adopted home be sound
I've married and have other children
and one thing they cannot fulfill
The place for you in my heart
which is still so very real
Yes, they know all about you
for my first child you will always be
And if and when we find you
their arms will be open you'll see
I hope that those who have loved you
and nourished you day after day
have made you feel very special
and for this I'll continue to pray

Regrets

I had a friend once tell me
her birthmother she'd never find
Because you changed pertinent information
this is where you crossed the line
She felt she had a right to know
something of her life from before
Unfortunately you broke her heart
with each request you chose to ignore
Did you think somehow this would change
the love she felt strongly for you
Mother how could you not know
that this would not be true
She told you she was devoted
to the family with which she lived
And loved dearly you and her father
because all to her you did give
You gave her love and affection
a happy home filled with care
But unfortunately in this one area
you found it difficult to be there
She said you'd discuss everything
that a mother and daughter could share
But when it came to knowing her past
you'd pretend it was not even there
She felt you even changed her birth date
in hopes of covering the trail
To go to such great lengths
it was her heart that you did fail
She left it alone for a while
and didn't bring it up for years
Because she came to realize
it would only cause more tears

She just couldn't understand
how a mom who could love her so
could allow her to live with such torment
As she felt her pain you did know
She made a last attempt on your death bed
when you were so very ill
She thought you'd share this last secret
that you knew would help her to heal
Sadly to say she's still hurting
because unbelievably something you did
You left this world without sharing
the information for a lifetime you hid
At the time your child was an adult
to share this information may have been tough
But so many years of wonderful memories
"Mom"— wasn't this time enough
It's unfortunate that you didn't realize
what a real need she had to know
This information could have helped
after you her mom had to go
It's sad to say now she questions
how a mother this life could depart
Holding such vital information
that could have healed your daughter's heart
If you had handled this differently
the outcome may not have turned out so wrong
And the need to find her birthmother
may not have been in her so....strong
I'm sorry dear Mother you left here
to go to your place of rest
Not knowing that with this information
she still would have loved you the best

Secrets

Those oh so painful secrets
that we have chosen to keep
Have created in our lives a division
that causes my heart to weep
It started out with one
of which you would not share
To tell me of the past
of which you could not bear
I thought that since you loved me
that somehow on that day
When questioning my beginning
you'd have so much to say
Instead the pain I felt
by what you had to say
that you would not disclose
any details from that day
You asked why is it important
You thought I should let it go
You made the decision for me
that I had no need to know
I ask was this decision for me
when you refused what I asked you to do
Or was this about your feelings
that my knowing was a threat to you
You've spent your life to raise me
that we might be very close
But when I needed your support
you weren't there when I needed you most
Because of this something happened
which I would not have chosen to do

A secret of my own
I've now had to keep from you
Well one little secret
has now turned into two
And I am saddened at this time
that I am not able to share this with you
I've located my birthmother
but this secret I must keep
Because the reality of you knowing
would now cause <u>you</u> to weep
You'd see this as a betrayal
of sharing my love with another
But she is only my friend
and you will always be "mother"
I'm trying hard to convince her
that the love we've shared was so deep
But I see in her mind she wonders
why this secret I must keep
I understand her confusion
about why this finding I cannot share
Because even I feel very cheated
that in this you would not be there
Your response put me in a predicament
where I could not share this with you
And it's unfortunate your first secret
has turned this now into two

What is Success

I am quite successful
in this life that I have made
But how would things have been different
if in your life I had stayed
I handle closing important deals
in my work each and every day
But did not have the courage
for in my child's life to stay
Regardless of what I accomplish
I feel I always fall short
even when I'm clearly winning
when out on the tennis court
I take off in my fancy car
And while idling at a light
I try to think of my success
but somehow it doesn't feel right
When my friends pat me on my back
and say what a great job I've done
I wonder if they would still say this
if they knew that I walked away from a son
I tell myself it doesn't matter
and avoid the thought as much as I can
But these memories come back to haunt me
of that day I didn't stand up as a man
Successful by everyone's standards
really does apply to me
But deep inside I cannot feel it
I ask myself how can this be
If I allow myself to just face it
I'm afraid of what might be true
It has everything my child to do with
the day I walked away from you

Would you ever forgive me
if I came back into your life
or would you say I am no longer needed
Because my decision caused you such strife
Would you still my child resent me
if I admitted I had been weak
Or would you tell me my excuses
You'd prefer to myself I should keep
When I ask myself what is success
Others think it is about what I do
But deep down I know I'll never feel this
until I've dealt with the "issue" of you
Yes, I've closed so many deals
again of which my partners are proud
But I still ask myself what if they knew
that I walked out on the life of a child
One thing I now know for sure
is "things" play a very small part
and what I need to feel successful
is the healing of a child's heart
I can now see, my child
what is necessary for me to do
I must drum up the courage
to go out in life to find you
I am afraid of your rejection
but I must do all that I can
To let you know that I your father
am ready to stand up and now be a man!

Chosen

So you say that you look different
yes my child this is true
But this fact has no bearing
on how we feel about you
Feel what's in our hearts
when you feel that you don't belong
Because to think that you're not one of us
I am glad to say that you're wrong
When we look at you each day
the only thing we can see
is a child who means so very much
to both your father and me
So don't let this little fact
Cause your thoughts to run wild
for it was never based on looks
When we chose you as our child

What is a Child

What is a child
a beautiful gift from God
Those tiny little fingers
and chubby little toes
Those inquiring little eyes
and kissable little nose
Those oh so perfect lips
and rounded little head
Those salty little tears
that sometimes must be shed
Those little arms for reaching
a tummy to be fed
Those kicking little legs
that always find your head
That fragile little body
that longs for us to hold
Remember they're God's gift
for us to love, shape and mold
If you are so blessed
to hold such a one in your arms
Remember it's your duty
to keep them away from harm
For there is no finer gift
that in your life you'll receive
Than to protect this little life
no finer task will you ever achieve

What is a Parent

You've accepted a task
a lifetime one you see
To raise these little angels
to be all that they can be
Yes, it is exciting
and truly so much fun
But when the times get tough
you'll know the real task has begun
It's so easy to love them
when they're small, babbling and drooling
But what about when they're older
and it's you they think they're fooling
There'll be hours of laughing
and playing on the floor
But what about when they're older
and slamming their bedroom door
It will be so rewarding
when they kiss and say you're nice
But what about that day
when they no longer seek your advice
Those quiet moments in the morning
when you would drive them to school
Have now abruptly stopped
because it's no longer cool
You had this excited little child
who loved going with you to a game
And now a hug in front of friends
would cause the ultimate shame
Well this my friend is a parent
someone mature, loving and wise

Who would not in these circumstances
that sweet child begin to despise
Yes, of course it might hurt
to feel in the relationship a wedge
but to these growing young children
they're just stepping out on the edge
Although we want to grab them
and for dear life to hold
It's your job as a parent
to let them step out of the fold
Just trust all that you've done
you've sown a powerful seed
This will always be with them
and they will one day take heed
The job of being a parent
is being wise enough to know
That they are still our children
and they need some space to grow
When they are yet teenagers
your relationship seems at its end
But when they become young adults
they can sometimes become your best friend
So remember this dear parent
when at the end of your rope
There are other parents out there
who can tell you there is still hope

Belonging

Who am I you ask
where do I belong
With those my child who love you
why does it feel so wrong
Is it because you're looking
for something that isn't there
That we couldn't possibly love you
because you we did not bear
Yes, your eyes might be different
and so might the color of your hair
But it's the love in our hearts
that you should really compare
Don't choose this nightmare of doubts
day after day to live
Please try to let your heart focus
on the love that we have to give
We sought so hard to find you
a child to love and raise
To show you patience and understanding
and to shower you with praise
And so our hearts are broken
and it truly makes us sad
To see you so unhappy
and constantly feeling bad
Don't let being adopted haunt you
and cause you so much strife
You are our child so wanted
and you can have a beautiful life
You have questions we know that need answers
and truly we do understand
But look at the positives sweetheart
and hold on tight to our hands
We'll walk with you through this
and help you to be strong
Because one thing we are sure of
is that this is where you belong

Friends

Our friends were all so happy
when we finally brought you home
We didn't get very much sleep
between your crying and answering the phone
We were sitting on cloud nine
for days and days on end
And each day would walk through the door
another well-wishing friend
They brought you adorable little outfits
in pinks, yellows and blues
and tons and tons of stuffed animals
and yes they were all for you
I realized one more thing
during those blissful days
that our friends were also there for you
and they showed this in so many ways
If something should ever happen
and for you there we cannot be
I would like to assure you
that our friends you may count on you see

Keep the Door Open

I asked an innocent question
why don't we look the same
Instead of a loving answer
your stern look caused me pain
That was when the wall started
building between you and me
Because I felt just by asking
you became insulted you see
Whenever I had future questions
I knew to put them on hold
Not to suffer the repercussions
of your anger and need to scold
In my teen years you said we're not close
this you couldn't seem to understand
Not realizing that early on
it was you who dealt "us" this hand
Maybe one day we'll recover
and we can talk about this some more
But that day can only come
when it's safe to unlock the door

Your Mommy

I knew I was your mommy
when your cries I was able to calm
And you would get so excited
eating cheerios right from my palm
I knew I was your mommy
when you wouldn't want me to leave
I'd pick you up and I'd hold you
as your tears would stain my sleeve
I knew I was your mommy
when you had an accident playing in the dirt
you needed me to kiss your finger
so that it would no longer hurt
I knew I was your mommy
When in dreams that monster'd appear
you'd say please sleep with me Mommy
He won't come back if you are here
I knew I was your mommy
when you shouted to me from your bed
Mommy there's no other mommy
I'd rather have instead
I knew I was your mommy
when I overheard you pray
Lord please bless my mommy
because I need her everyday

Growing Pains

When you're feeling somewhat isolated
your adoption please don't blame
Because there are birth children
who often feel the same
We all sometimes feel in our lives
that we don't know where we belong
But to blame it on your adoption
this I feel would be wrong
Take a look around at your friends
who have struggles of their own
You'll see it's a part of life
and not about how they came to their home
I think its sometimes easy
to place blame on an obvious choice
It has to be because I'm different
you keep hearing from this little voice
My child we are all different
each in our own little way
So when things really start to bother you
just take out some time to pray
I know that God will show you
the answers that you seek
And know that being adopted
is not a sign of being weak
Adoption is not a handicap
in any way, shape or form
So know the struggles you're feeling
are just a part of the norm
Keep your heart and mind open
and I know that you will see
That the things that you question
are not affected by how you came to be
We all must search and find ourselves
and decide in which direction we'll go
Just keep pressing forward
and I promise one day that you'll know
Adoption is a blessing
as being birthed into a family is too
so these growing pains you are feeling
are just a road map to becoming you!

Journey

I could only imagine
when embarking upon this journey,
What this would mean —
would you really love us?

Would we raise you the proper way
Would we be able to calm your fears
and know the right things to say
We now must admit to you
we wondered how long it would take
to truly love and bond with you
this child whom we did not make
We wondered about your height
would you be short or tall
and even though we wondered
it made no difference at all
We wondered if you would be happy
that you were adopted into our home
Or would you someday say
you wish we had left you alone
Would we be good parents
of which you would be proud
Or would you one day look at us
and say I am not your child
Even though there were fears
on both our parts you see
we still took the journey
so our family could come to be
I can only tell you, darling
having you exceeded all our dreams
And it only took a few seconds
for everything to us you would mean
We would not trade this journey
or have done it any other way
because of the bond that was made
with you on that very first day

Through My Eyes

I'm so glad that you were there for me
a child with special needs you would take
I knew that you had to be special
and wonderful parents you'd make
Yes, this was quite a tall order
but to make sure I wouldn't grow up alone
although you knew there would be challenges
you still loved me and gave me a home
You knew you would need to feed me
and clean me up every day
and the older I became
you knew this would not go away
Because I was not born perfect
I had a few problems you see
but that did not deter you
from providing a home for me
You looked into your heart
and reached for something so deep
enough love for you to share with me
although the road you knew would be steep
Oh how selfless of you
to open widely your door
and all my little imperfections
you just kindly chose to ignore
Instead, what really mattered
was something you saw in my eyes
I needed someone to love me
and to help calm my cries
I know there will be some things
that in life I can never do
But that will just leave more room
in my heart to truly love you

Although, I may never be strong enough
to wrap you tightly in my arms
I hope my eyes will show
that I know you've kept me from harm
Although it is difficult to verbalize,
or articulate all that I feel
I hope my eyes can show you
that my love for you is so real
Sometimes others may think
I'm not aware of what's going on
But I would like to assure you
this is where they are wrong
I can feel something so special
when you bundle me and tie up my hood
that the person who's standing before me
is here to do me some "good"
I'm so glad you chose to love me
and on your heart strings I was able to pull
So although my abilities are limited
your love has made my life so full
On those days when you are tired
because of all you've done for me
know your love and unyielding dedication
Through my eyes I can clearly see!

Tough Choices

There is a little story
to you that I must tell
About the time I lost you
my life was a living hell
My parents knew my dilemma
and left me very little choice
In the decision about your adoption
I had very little voice
Oh how much I hated them
for the decision that was made
And I want you to know
that they paid and paid and paid
But now that I am older
through experiences I can now see
That the decision was not to punish
but to help both you and me
It gave me the chance to grow
and do positive things with my life
And to get rid of all the anger
hatred, turmoil and strife
I hope for you my child
this decision brought you little pain
And you were placed with caring parents
who truly knew what they had gained
A beautiful child for loving
who would certainly grow up to be
One well-rounded, strong and confident
for the entire world to see
I have forgiven my parents
we have all become very close
It's your happiness wherever you are
that we all truly pray for the most
If one day we should meet
and I do hope that day will come
I hope you will have no ill feelings
about what years ago had to be done

Job Well Done

You've assured me since I was a baby
that I was your very own
You promised me my whole life
that you would never leave me alone
You showered me with your love
and showed me what made a home so real
It was because of all these things
that truly blessed I did feel
I had someone to count on
when in life I had questions or doubts
Who was always there to comfort me
and not during these times to shout
I had you there to cheer for me
in all I set out to do
and when my ability I would question
I'd look in the crowd for you
I saw in the distance your face
that said be the best you can be
and whether you win or lose
you're already a winner to me
You came to my school functions
when there you were so very proud
you said to all who would listen
you see that one — she is my child
The pride that I saw in your face
with each task I set out to do
removed from my heart any doubts
of my belonging to you
I need to tell you today
because of all of your backing
that life for me was so full
and I felt nothing was lacking
If you ever need a referral
for a job you have done very well
just send them to me your daughter
for I have a story to tell
It's about a wonderful parent
and all the things that you knew to do
to make my life so special
when as a baby I came unto you
You supported me throughout my lifetime
and guided me through all I've tried to do
I'd like to tell you dear parent
that because of this I truly love you!

In Time

This my child is a promise
that we will now make to you
That if you feel the need to search
we will help you to see it through
Any information we may have
that we feel you need to know
We promise to share it with you
after we have helped you to grow
The timing is so important
when this information we give
We want you to know all the details
once you have had a chance to live
We want you to know who you are
and not just from where you came
We want you to choose your own life
and not circumstances to blame
We'll be available to you for discussions
over time as you continue to grow
But before opening any doors
there is something we need you to know
There are so many possibilities
of what you might actually find
We just want you to be aware
when you play this over in your mind
The news could be great and exciting
and everything you'd want to hear
But things could be quite the opposite
and we just want you prepared my dear
We'll cross that bridge when we reach it
and we know that all will be fine
Because we'll be right there with you
if you'll trust us to know when it's time

Partnership

Well today I got into trouble
because I came home with a "C"
Wait before you get upset
there is something to know about me
I'm a very smart little kid
an "A" student I guess you could say
You had no idea you bore a genius
back on that special day
Thank you for my beginning
when inside you held me dear
You fed, protected and loved me
until I was delivered here
It's okay I really don't blame you
for the choice that you made
You carried me safely for nine months
so your price you have already paid
For without you I couldn't have seen
all the joy that adoption could bring
I have two super parents
yes who make me cross every "T"
But I know you would probably love them
because they truly love me

Real Mother

*W*hen I said that I was adopted
I was shocked by your reply
you said "I am so sorry"
I stepped back and wondered why
you said "Your mom didn't want you"
Oh what a very sad fate
I thought what are you saying
my life has truly been great
Please don't be sorry
for what you think I must feel
Let me educate you a little
on what makes a mother so real
A mother is one who loves you
and tends to all of your needs
It really has little to do with
who actually carried the seed
When I was sick with an illness
she put me right in her bed
And all night long if needed
she'd gladly rub my head
When someone hurt my feelings
I did not cry alone
My mother also shed
a few tears of her own
When I was a little older
and had my very first kiss
She didn't begin to scold me
but said just remember this
The first kiss is exciting
This I know is true
but remember you are a lady
so be careful of what you do
She said love my darling
is such a beautiful thing
But save the very best
until you're married and wearing a ring
Now if this doesn't sound like a mother
I don't know what else I can say
A mom is the one in my corner
who is there for me each and every day
My friend when you think of real moms
what I need for you to see
Is my mom is the one who has labored
to help me be all I can be

Knowledge

If a child were a cardiologist
they'd need to know all the parts
And very intricate details
of their patients' hearts
If a child were a good mechanic
they'd be expected to know
All the parts to a car
in order to make it go
So when a child comes to you
to question their start
it's because sometimes they feel
they need that missing part
To complete the puzzle
of the story of their life
It's not to upset you
or cause you any strife
I know that this subject
brings up mixed emotions
and dealing with this issue
is not just a notion
You may say to yourselves
we don't think they should know
Let's just keep them to ourselves
and we'll just watch them grow
Well I tell you this decision
would be okay too
As long as the child
doesn't ask this of you
But if they should ask
don't close that door
Talk to them kindly
about what came before

We've often wondered
if we'd been afraid
would concealing this information
destroy the life we've made
Therefore, when we weighed it
we found this to be true
To deny them this knowledge
can push them away from you
Don't get us wrong
there is an appropriate time
Just let your children know this
just to ease their minds
Remember this dear parents
if this thought makes you blue
If your relationship is strong
nothing can take them from you

The Promise

We look at you this baby
who is so beautiful you see
We sit back and we wonder
what do you think he'll be
A doctor or a lawyer
for we cannot yet say
For it's your choice our child
but we'll help you along the way
We'll love, protect and nurture
that you might grow big and strong
We will also try to minimize
the things that could go wrong
We will answer all of your questions
and try to calm all of your fears
And let you know that we love you
even through the difficult years
When you came into our lives
a promise to you we did swear
To love, protect and nurture
this child who we did not bear

Letting Go

I tried so hard to hide
what I knew others would one day see
The child that I was carrying
would soon be delivered to me
I didn't try to hide this
of you I was not ashamed
I only thought it best
because I wouldn't be choosing your name
I had my mind made up
adoption was the way I must go
This is why my child
I wanted no one to know
I felt that they might judge me
as I'm afraid one day you will too
But my decision was truly made
out of what I felt best for you
No one can understand
what goes through a birthmother's head
And the many, many tears
that at night were shed in my bed
Until they've been in my place
it would be impossible to know
What I felt for you child
when I decided to let go
I wanted for you the very best
that at the time I could not give
I was sorting out my own life
and wondering how I would live
I did not have a real place
for me that I could call home
I could not do this to you child
and have you grow up all alone
I'm hoping one day to meet you
and hope you might understand
I did the very best I could
'til on my feet I was able to stand

Something We Share

I stand in line next to you
and although you see me there
You have no way of knowing
there's something in common we share
Your child looks different from you
this I can clearly see
And I have a child by my side
who actually looks like me
You frown when you see me watching
thinking how rude I am sure
But what you don't really know
is I know what you've had to endure
The praying and the waiting
wondering if a child to you would come
And how life at times seemed unbearable
while waiting for that little one
I felt a little sad
because my heart out to you did go
but I didn't have the nerve
to tell you what I wanted you to know
The next time you see someone watching
this might be of help to you
To know it might be another mother
who has adopted her little one too

One of Us

To our families we'd like to say thank you
for treating our child as your own
She was never made to feel isolated
ostracized or alone
From the first day that you saw her
in your arms her you took
There was never any difference
in a word, a question, a look
Dear parents you treated her kindly
to our siblings you all did too
You said we promise to love her
as though she came from you
To you it made no difference
how this child was conceived
because today in this family
she has now been received
We want for this little baby
nothing but the very best
Know that throughout her lifetime
she'll be treated like all the rest

Boundaries

People are always asking
they say how can this be
They always seem to question
the relationship between you and me
They say how is it possible
to share this child with another
How confusing that must be
to take advice from the other mother
Life must sometimes get difficult
when on a decision we cannot agree
They say if I'm the sole provider
the final say should fall to me
I explain this is not a battle
where the strongest will survive
This is about raising a child
who because of you today is alive
And so for that I thank you
for this child you've given me to raise
And rather than question your involvement
your unselfishness they should praise
I told them we both know the boundaries
the well-being of our child is at stake
So in trying to do this job together
limited mistakes we sometimes make
You are most often respectful
and stand behind the decisions we make
You are not in our child's life
for our place to try to take
You just want him to know you
and most importantly to know
that you too his mother loves him
even though you had to let go

Memories

There were nights when I stood
and looked down at you in bed
I rubbed your beautiful curls
that were all over your head
I had the urge to hum
a sweet little lullabye
If you had opened your eyes
you'd probably have wondered why
You were already sleeping
and probably counting sheep
but to see this sweet life before me
brought up feelings which caused me to weep
I often took those moments
when you were lying in your bed
to think of the day we were blessed with you
and the day you'll leave home I'll dread
I want to hold you forever
and my baby you'll always be
I know sometimes it's annoying
but please be patient with me
Please don't make me promise
that when you're 16 and lying in bed
That I will not have the privilege
of rubbing your sweet little head

Reasons

Did they not love me
Is what you said to me
I said of course they did
then how'd this adoption come to be
Sometimes in our lives
we are young and make mistakes
And sometimes these judgments
Cause us difficult decisions to make
They were two very young people
who moved too quickly you see
They were not really sure
if tomorrow a couple they'd be
Although they felt too young
to see this position through
they asked God to help them
to do what was best for you
They were determined to find a couple
who would both treat you like gold
Someone to cherish and love you
and their beautiful child to hold
This decision didn't come easily
and they wanted you to know
it wasn't because they didn't love you
that they decided to let you go
They wanted for you a family
where both parents there would be
Who would love, protect and cherish you
and that's how you came to me
They placed you with our family
not to try to take their place
but to raise you as our child
with true love, kindness and grace

The Ultimate Sacrifice

When you search your life
and feel nothing you have done
Please do think again
about that little one
If it had not been for you
a child I would not have gained
Please let this bit of knowledge
help to ease your pain
The life of a child
is life's most precious gift
So when down on yourself
please do remember this
What it took on that day
for this life for you to give
I hope the sacrifice will sustain you
for as long as you shall live
People give gifts of diamonds
and even silver and gold
But not one of these can replace
this beautiful life I hold
So if someone should ever say
what in life did you ever do
You stand up proudly and reply
I gave a life how about you

We'll Go the Distance

If you should ever question
our complete devotion to you
Let us tell you the story
of all that we went through
To bring you to our home
to live both safe and sound
We chose to go much further
than our homeland ground
We traveled overseas
and even slept on floors
To see to it our child
that our home would become yours
It was all so very foreign
and the accents strange to hear
But they became music to our ears
when to us you did appear
We wished to leave immediately
to get you where you belonged
And we prayed 'til we returned
that nothing would go wrong
When traveling with you home
back to our homeland soil
We knew this precious child
we'd spend our lives to spoil
We hope through this story
that you can clearly see
if you should ever need us
you know right where we'll be
This our child we feel
was the least that we could do
and whatever happens in your life
we'll go the distance for you

It's Not Always Easy

You are now a teenager
and we have watched you grow
It hasn't all been easy
as of course you already know
Some yelling and some screaming
a few doors that have been slammed
But we will all get through this
I truly know we can
Today you tried to hurt us
with something you angrily said
That we are not your real parents
and you wish that we were dead
I just stared at you for a moment
through my anguish and pain
And said we still love you
and would adopt you all over again
Because we hope deep inside
you know our child what is true
That all we've done in your life
has all been to benefit you

Welcome Back

You said when you're eighteen you're leaving
that you are so out of here!
You're going off to find
your "other" mother dear
We hope that when you find her
the truth that you would tell
We only tried to love you
though your life you thought was hell
When you were heartbroken
it was you who pulled away
Although we tried to help you
you heard nothing we had to say
We tried to do all the things
we thought were really the best
But you only shouted constantly
how we made your whole life a mess
You always had this feeling
the grass would be greener on the other side
When all we wanted to instill
was a healthy sense of pride
We can only hope for you
that you find what you're looking for
But if the grass is not greener
you are welcome back at our door

Thank You

*H*ello birthmother
there is something I must say
did you ever think you'd hear from me
The adoptive mother one day
I have some things to share with you
that I thought you might like to know
I thought of you so often
while watching our child grow
I said Lord would you please bless her
wherever she may be
And let her know I cherish
this gift she gave to me
Give her peace in her heart
that her child is out of harm's way
In spite of what she sees
on the news each and everyday
On our child's birthday
a prayer for you we'd share
And ask for God to bless you
and let you know how much we care
For this beautiful child
who was made possible to us through you
You do not need to worry
we'll see our responsibilities through
Another thing I must tell you
she's loved by family, neighbors and friends
She is a child you'd be proud of
and for this I thank you again
This child has brought so much joy
into our lives everyday
and when I look in her eyes
I can't help but for you to pray

Trust your heart...

The heart is very loyal in that it will let us know when a matter is unsettled. Although, in our heads we try to convince ourselves that there is no conflict, our hearts will keep bringing a matter to the forefront of our minds seeking resolution. It has the unique ability not to allow us total peace until we are true to ourselves as well as to others. Listen to your heart - it is the truest friend you will ever have.

S. Mills

ACKNOWLEDGEMENTS

I would first like to give thanks to God who gave me the inspiration to start this project. I am thankful for the wisdom and knowledge imparted unto me to see this work through to completion. I am thankful for the love and compassion that I have always felt for others which was without a doubt instrumental in helping me capture the feelings of those who may have had a different role than myself in the adoption process.

I would like to thank my wonderful husband, Terry. Whenever, I said "I have a vision of doing..." even though you knew it might involve financial costs or the sharing of my time, you always supported me. You have been a wonderful partner. I can't thank you enough for the support and the confidence you have shown in me.

To my mom, thank you, when I was little you let me know not only was it okay to dream, but, it was okay to really believe in those dreams. Whenever I'd say "Mom, when I get big I'm going to ..." You'd look at me and say "Yes, I'm sure you will." (smile) It was your believing in me that made it easy to believe in myself. You are "the best", and I am proud that you are my mom.

I'd like to thank my father for teaching me at a very young age to be happy for others. He always taught us not to envy or begrudge anyone their successes in life. His philosophy is that if people would take the same energy used to begrudge or envy others and apply it toward following their own dreams - not only would they succeed, but they could feel good about it when they got there. Dad, I have always remembered this. I want you to know that this was very instrumental in the positive attitude that I have tried to maintain throughout my life.

I would like to thank my cheerleader, my sister Lynn. You would always dream for me even when you wouldn't dream for yourself. Whatever I'd do or accomplish in life you always let me know that there is more to do. Thank you for always putting me on a pedestal; but, I want you to know that you deserve for "yourself" every dream that you have wished for me.

To my brother John, and my nieces and nephews — you all mean so much to me. I hope you too will follow your dreams.

My list would not be complete if I didn't thank my extended family members who have believed in me and let me know it throughout my life.

To my largest support system of all, "my friends" — you have all made my life so full. Your dedication, encouraging words, time, support and love have been overwhelming. So many of you have told me what my being in your life has meant to you; your being in my life has been a priceless gift to me. I could write another book just on the ways that you have all touched my life. Please let this poem that I have written sum it up for now:

Sincere and loving friends
are worth their weight in gold,
It really doesn't matter
if the friendship is new or old,
What really is important
is from each other - what we can expect,
honesty, kindness and loyalty
for the hearts of "true" friends to connect!

Brittany Press
P.O. Box 10
Carmel, Indiana
46082

Send me _____ copies of *Reflections of Adoption* at $13.95 per copy.

Enclosed is my check or money order for $_____.

     Name _____

     Address _____

     City _____State___Zip code_____

Shipping $3.50 for the first book and $1.00 for each additional book.

Indiana residents add 5% sales tax.

     Make checks payable to: Brittany Press

For any inquiries please contact:

       Brittany Press
       P.O. Box 10
       Carmel, IN 46082
          or
       www.BrittanyPress.com
       Giftadp@aol.com